D1582697

SCOTLAND

Cullen House

Provost Skene's House
Aberdeen

Crathes

St Mary's, Grandtully

Stobhall

Huntingtower

Earlshall

Falkland Palace

Stirling Castle

Culross Palace

Kirkcaldy

Aberdour Castle

Kinneil House

Northfield
Prestongrange
Pinkie House Musselburgh

Edinburgh

Skelmorlie Aisle
Largs

Traquair House

Open to the public

Not open to the public

Location of
Painted Renaissance
Decoration

THE
PAINTED CEILINGS
OF SCOTLAND

1550-1650

By M. R. APTED, MA, PhD, FSA

Inspector of Ancient Monuments

EDINBURGH

HER MAJESTY'S STATIONERY OFFICE

1966

The frontispiece shows the astral ceiling at Cullen House, Banffshire

Contents

v

Plates

The design on the dust jacket is taken from the bedroom ceiling at Earlshall (Plate 33)
The cover device is a detail from Stobhall (page 8, Plate 77)
Small drawings in the text are from Crathes (title page, pages 34, 68, 76, 88, 94), Northfield (page xvi), Rossend Castle (decorative borders) and Skelmorlie Aisle (pages 26, 106)
The endpaper maps show the location of outstanding examples of mediaeval and renaissance painted decoration in Scotland

Acknowledgements

The painted decoration illustrated in this book was recorded by the kind permission of the owners of the buildings concerned. Line drawings are by Mr. T. Borthwick, ceiling surveys by Miss Thea McDonald and photographs by Mr. J. Pugh, AIIP, ARPS.

Photographs of the Palace of Holyroodhouse are reproduced by gracious permission of Her Majesty The Queen and Plates 80-82 by courtesy of the British Museum. Plate 67 has been copied from *Early Bible Illustrations* by James Strachan. Plate 16 is from the library of the Scottish National Buildings Record.

The survey of painted decoration was based initially on Robert Brydall's *History of Art in Scotland* (1889) and on the descriptions of individual ceilings in the *Proceedings of the Society of Antiquaries of Scotland* and the *Inventories of the Royal Commission on Ancient Monuments*.

Foreword

This book is an introduction to the painted ceilings which were popular in Scotland during the reign of James VI and for about a generation thereafter. It is not exhaustive since there are something like a hundred known examples, but it illustrates the best and shows where they are to be found, how they were made and when and (occasionally) by whom they were painted. It ends with a note on the problems of conservation.

The paintings were not intended to be works of art (wall paper is the modern equivalent) but were painted by skilled craftsmen with great fluency —sometimes beautiful, often entertaining and always a first-hand record of taste and ideas. In terms of painted decoration Scotland after the Reformation was not the dour and sober place one might imagine.

Such decoration was not peculiar to Scotland. All over Europe in the late sixteenth century buildings of stone and timber and even temporary pavilions of canvas were lavishly painted. Much of this decoration has been destroyed, but in Scotland the plastered ceilings of tower-houses often conceal decoration untouched since it was painted some three centuries ago. Such painting has therefore an international as well as a local significance.

*Buildings containing notable examples of painted interior decoration
which are open to the public*

MEDIAEVAL

Berwickshire	Dryburgh Abbey*
Fife	Inchcolm Abbey*
Orkney	St. Magnus Cathedral, Kirkwall†
West Lothian	Torphichen Preceptory*

LATER MEDIAEVAL

Aberdeenshire	St. Machar's Cathedral†
Angus	Church of Foulis Easter†
Angus	Guthrie Castle†
Fife	Dunfermline Abbey*
Perthshire	Dunkeld Cathedral*

RENAISSANCE

Aberdeenshire	Provost Skene's House, Aberdeen (Museum)
Ayrshire	Largs, Skelmorlie Aisle*
Banffshire	Cullen House†
Fife	Aberdour Castle*
Fife	Culross Palace* (National Trust)
Fife	Falkland Palace† (National Trust)
Kincardineshire	Crathes† (National Trust)
Midlothian	Edinburgh Castle*
Midlothian	Palace of Holyroodhouse*
Peeblesshire	Traquair House†
Perthshire	Huntingtower*
Perthshire	St. Mary's Church, Grandtully*
Stirlingshire	Chapel Royal, Stirling Castle*
West Lothian	Kinneil House, Bo'ness*

NOTE: Buildings marked (*) are under the guardianship of the Ministry of Public Building and Works
Those marked (†) are either churches in use or privately owned buildings open to the public at stated times

xiv

The Painted Ceilings of Scotland
1550-1650

CHAPTER ONE

Painted decoration before 1550

LITTLE mediaeval painting can be seen in Scotland today since few buildings of the period are sufficiently intact to preserve it, but enough survives to show that it did exist. The earliest example is a single painted arch-stone or voussoir displayed under a glass case in the nave of Glasgow Cathedral. The palm-leaf type of decoration on this stone has not been found anywhere else in Scotland, but a similar design was used in Durham Cathedral about 1175 and the Glasgow example is believed to be a surviving fragment of the cathedral dedicated by Jocelin, bishop of Glasgow, in 1197.

Other early examples were probably all painted in the thirteenth century and consist, with one exception, of simple patterns in primary colours or of painted imitations of coursed masonry known as ashlar. The best preserved scheme of this kind, which can be studied in some detail on a bright, dry day, is in the late thirteenth century chapter-house at Dryburgh Abbey where there has been a painted arcade on the walls, painted decoration round the windows and imitation ashlar on the vault. There are also traces of painting in the sacristy and in the north transept of the abbey church. There is evidence of another extensive scheme in St. Magnus Cathedral, Kirkwall, where nave, transepts and choir were all painted and where it is still possible to reconstruct some of the patterns on windows, arches and vaulting ribs; at the end of the last century decoration was also visible on the great pillars of the nave. Elsewhere there are ill-preserved patterns at Pluscarden and Dunfermline, painted ashlar at Arbroath and Torphichen and part of a processional scene on the back of a tomb recess at Inchcolm—the only known example of mediaeval figure painting.

The only contemporary domestic painted decoration is to be seen on a vault rib excavated from the ditch at Dirleton Castle, now in the castle museum, which has been painted with broad chevrons in alternating colours.

Rather more ecclesiastical decoration survives from the years 1450-1550, usually in buildings of the same period. Two outstanding examples survive, both from the end of the fifteenth century and possibly by the same hand, one in the former collegiate church of Foulis Easter near Dundee, the other at Guthrie Castle about twelve miles further to the north-east. At Foulis the paintings are well preserved and, with the exception of a Trinity painting, formerly associated with a rood screen and loft; there are small panels with the figures of Christ, apostles and martyrs from the parapet and a large Crucifixion scene on boards which originally filled the space between loft and roof. At one time there were paintings on the wall plaster as well, but these have disappeared. At Guthrie the scenes are painted on a wooden vault from the family burial aisle which has now been cut up into sections and mounted on the walls of the castle hall. One side of the vault illustrated the Crucifixion and the other Judgement Day. The latter is the better preserved; it is still possible to distinguish the figure of Christ seated on a rainbow with Mary and John the Baptist kneeling before Him in intercession for the dead who are rising from their graves and passing before Our Lord in judgement on their way to either heaven or hell. Other examples of church painting of the period are to be seen in Dunfermline Abbey, Dunkeld Cathedral and Pluscarden Priory, but no contemporary domestic decoration has been identified.

Many church furnishings of the same period were also painted. The most important surviving examples are the two panels from the Collegiate Church of the Holy Trinity, Edinburgh, believed to have been painted by the Dutch artist Van der Goes about 1480, now on exhibition in the National Gallery of Scotland. There are also painted choir stalls from Lincluden in the National Museum of Antiquities.

It is unlikely that mediaeval painting would have been regarded as of any interest in the second half of the sixteenth century, but there may have been some continuity between the ecclesiastical decoration which preceded the

Reformation and the domestic decoration that followed it. To a minor extent this is demonstrated by a painter such as Walter Binning who in 1544 was painting processional statues for the Hammermen of Edinburgh and in 1550 domestic decoration for the Regent Arran, or by the fact that the Judgement of Solomon is to be seen on the walls both of the fifteenth century tower of Dunkeld Cathedral and of the 1611 range of Culross Palace. In more general terms the Reformation may even have encouraged the spread of domestic decoration since the loss of church patronage and the redistribution of wealth may have set craftsmen free to undertake domestic painting and have provided the means for their employment. Whether this was the case or not, it is clear that decorative painting as such was not a sixteenth century innovation.

PLATES ILLUSTRATING CHAPTER ONE

1. Dryburgh Abbey, Berwickshire: chapter-house
2. Dryburgh Abbey: chapter-house arcade
3. Dryburgh Abbey: chapter-house vault
4. Church of Foulis Easter, Angus: Crucifixion
5. Foulis Easter: panels from west parapet of rood loft
6. Guthrie Castle, Angus: Christ in Majesty
7. Dunfermline Abbey, Fife: painted vault

out). Painted arcades on the side walls match the stone arcade on the end wall. The stone vault is masked by painted masonry. Thirteenth century. Plate 2 (*below, left*) Dryburgh Abbey; chapter-house arcade showing detail of the end wall and painted arcade. Arches enclose geometrical patterns and conventional foliage. Plate 3 (*below, right*) Dryburgh Abbey; chapter-house vault. Small rectangles of painted masonry conceal larger blocks of real stone underneath. Simple patterns define window surrounds

5

PAINTED DECORATION BEFORE 1550: Plate **6** Guthrie Castle, Angus; Christ in Majesty. A detail from 'Doom', a popular mediaeval subject showing the risen dead facing Our Lord in judgement before passing to heaven or hell. Late fifteenth century. Plate **7** (*below*) Dunfermline Abbey, Fife; painted vault, north aisle. St. Paul, St. Andrew and St. Peter. Sixteenth century. Patterns on vaulting ribs may survive from earlier decorative scheme

CHAPTER TWO

Where the painted ceilings are found

ROYAL PALACES

At the end of the sixteenth century the principal royal residences in Scotland were at Linlithgow, Dunfermline, Edinburgh (Palace of Holyroodhouse and Edinburgh Castle), Stirling and Falkland. Linlithgow and Dunfermline are now in ruin, but the remainder survive sufficiently to show that painted decoration was a feature in the palaces of the period.

Historically the most interesting survival is the timber ceiling in Queen Mary's ante-room at Holyroodhouse which was put up in either 1558 or 1559 and is one of the few features in the palace today with which the queen can have been familiar. Strictly speaking it falls outside the scope of the present study because the coats of arms were carved in the round before being fixed in position and painted, but the somewhat similar arms in the bedroom next door were painted direct on to the ceiling. There was also a painted frieze incorporating the Honours of Scotland (crown, sword and sceptre) running right round both rooms.

Of almost equal historic interest is the painting in the little room at Edinburgh Castle in which James VI is said to have been born (1566). It includes the royal arms, the date of birth and a metrical prayer calling for Christ's blessing on the royal child and his successors. The ceiling is decorated with the monograms of Mary and James and with the thistles of Scotland.

9

At Stirling the royal apartments, hall and chapel were all once painted and some decoration, including a frieze, survives in the chapel of 1594. There is also painted decoration on the coffered ceiling in the chapel at Falkland consisting, like that in Queen Mary's bedroom, largely of the coats of arms and monograms of members of the royal family.

There is evidence that heraldic and other special features on the external facades of royal palaces were also painted as at Stirling where there are traces of the royal cipher over the chapel windows and at Linlithgow where fragments of paint have been found on the carvings of the windows in the 'new work' (i.e. the north wing, rebuilt for James VI in 1620). This is confirmed by a contract of 1629 for the chapel royal at Stirling which stipulates that 'the window heads, the ciphers and crowns with the off-sets' were to be 'new gilded and layed over with oil colour' and by an account for Linlithgow of the same year for 'painting and laying over with oil colour and for gilting with gold the whole fore face of the new work with the timber windows and window boards, stone windows and crownells, with a board for the king's arms'. The Linlithgow account includes details of the scaffolding. Twenty poles were brought from the town on February 7th and set up on the east side of the new work: on March 2nd they were transferred to the west side, on the 9th set up round the central stair and on the 24th returned to the town.

The royal arms over the gateways at the royal palaces were also painted. The most interesting example of this occurs at Falkland. In May 1629 John Robinson in Stirling was paid for the hire of a horse 'that carried a case with three boards in it whereon the king's arms is from Stirling to Falkland' and for a second horse for the painter who received £60 'for the painting of the foresaid three great boards and furnishing colours, gold, oil and the whole stuff thairto and for over-laying and marbling the three housings above the great gate where they stand'. The housings can still be seen over the entry at Falkland but the existing heraldic panels are modern. The painter employed at Falkland on this occasion was Valentine Jenkin who also worked for the King at Holyrood and Stirling. Payments for horse hire were often made to painters to enable them to travel with their equipment from one task to another.

Royal Palaces

8. Holyroodhouse, Edinburgh
9. Edinburgh Castle: birthplace of James VI. Painted frieze and ceiling
10. Holyroodhouse: painted frieze in Queen Mary's bedroom
11. Holyroodhouse: ceiling in Queen Mary's bedroom
12. Falkland, Fife: chapel ceiling
13. Falkland: chapel. Original screen and ceiling

Castles, Mansions and Houses

14. Huntingtower, Perthshire. Home of the
Earl of Gowrie and scene of the Raid of Ruthven
15. Aberdour Castle, Fife. Built for the Earls of Morton
16. Craigston Castle, Aberdeenshire
17. Culross Palace, Fife
18. Mary Somerville's House, Burntisland, Fife
19. John Knox House, Edinburgh
20. Lawnmarket, Edinburgh

Churches

21. Skelmorlie Aisle, Largs, Ayrshire
22. Skelmorlie Aisle: interior
23. Skelmorlie Aisle: 'Winter'
24. Skelmorlie Aisle: painted timber vault
25. St. Mary's Church, Grandtully, Perthshire
26. St. Mary's, Grandtully: painted vault

building on right. Considerably altered inside and out, but contains early decoration on the second floor. Plate 9 (*below, left*) Edinburgh Castle; birthplace of James VI. Painted frieze and ceiling. Modern panelling. Plate 10 (*below, right*) Holyroodhouse; painted frieze in Queen Mary's bedroom. The room was first plastered and painted in grey, black and white and subsequently panelled. Door, fireplace and present floor level are part of late seventeenth century alterations

13

ROYAL PALACES: Plate **11** (*above*) Holyroodhouse; ceiling in Queen Mary's bedroom. Erected for James VI and painted for Charles I. Arms and monograms of the royal family. Plate **12** (*below*), Falkland, Fife; chapel ceiling. A sixteenth century ceiling with seventeenth century decoration. Royal coats of arms and the lily, the thistle and the rose

CASTLES, MANSIONS AND HOUSES

The fashion for painted decoration was geographically and socially widespread. It extended from Dumfries in the south to Kirkwall on the mainland of Orkney in the north, with Edinburgh and Aberdeen probably the main centres of distribution; it enriched the homes of great nobles, provincial lairds, merchants and craftsmen alike.

The best-preserved examples of patronage on a grand scale are at Pinkie House, home of the Earl of Dunfermline, Lord Chancellor of Scotland, and Kinneil, palace of the Regent Arran. The homes of the Earl of Gowrie (Huntingtower), the Marquis of Huntly (Huntly Castle) and the Earl of Morton (Aberdour Castle) were also painted. There are striking and colourful examples of open timber ceilings at Crathes and Stobhall and an entertaining coved ceiling at Cullen House, including an elaborate representation of the siege of Troy. In almost every case the ceilings which survive were formerly associated with others that have been destroyed.

The biggest concentration of town-houses with painted decoration was in Edinburgh where lofty buildings like Gladstone's Land and the tenement facing it (now the county police headquarters) were painted internally on every important floor. Some of these buildings, such as John Knox House, were the homes of prosperous craftsmen or merchants. Outside Edinburgh there are examples of painting in many of the small burghs along the Fife coast. At Burntisland the restoration of Mary Somerville's House, originally the home of a merchant captain, led to the discovery of painted decoration on the top floor. At Kirkcaldy painted decoration can still be seen in the old house by the harbour known as Sailor's Walk. Best-known of all is the so-called Culross Palace, mansion of Sir George Bruce, a royal favourite who made a fortune from salt and coal. The interiors are lined with wood, once lavishly painted—there were formerly at least eight painted rooms as well as painted staircases and lobbies. Paintings have also been recorded in Dundee and Linlithgow and there is still an interesting example to be seen in Provost Skene's House, Aberdeen, now preserved as a period museum. This house also contains a unique example of the landscape type of decoration popular in the eighteenth century, the panels in one room being marbled and the enclosing frames painted with figures and miniature landscapes in the Italian manner.

7 (an attempt to kidnap James VI, 1582). One ceiling (an early example) survives in the east (right) tower, with traces of painting elsewhere

CASTLES, MANSIONS AND HOUSES: Plate **15** (*above*) Aberdour Castle, Fife. Built for the Earls of Morton. Painted ceiling in projecting stair-tower (right). The long gallery (*c.* 1632), damaged by fire in the seventeenth century, may also have been painted. Plate **16** (*below*) Craigston Castle, Aberdeenshire. One of the fine tower-houses of North East Scotland. It once contained painted ceilings of which fragments are preserved in the stable. Vaulting ribs are painted under the great arch, a rare example of external decoration

CASTLES, MANSIONS AND HOUSES: Plate 17 (*above*) Culross Palace, Fife. So called because built palace-wise, i.e. horizontally rather than vertically. The most elaborately decorated small mansion known in Scotland (1597-1611). Plate 18 (*below*) Mary Somerville's House, Burntisland, Fife. Built for a family of merchants and ship owners, and occupied in the late eighteenth century by the famous astronomer whose name was given to Oxford's first college for women. Two painted rooms divided by a wooden partition once occupied the top floor. 17th century

CASTLES, MANSIONS AND HOUSES:
Plate **19** (*left*) John Knox House, Edinburgh. The stone front was built for James Mosman (Edinburgh goldsmith executed as a supporter of Queen Mary, 1573). Painted ceiling on the second floor. Plate **20** (*below*) Lawnmarket, Edinburgh. Two frontages which once formed a single building with an open arcade at street level. All rooms on the first and second floors were formerly painted (*c.* 1620)

CHURCHES: Plate **21** (*right*) Skelmorlie Aisle, Largs, Ayrshire. The burial aisle (added the parish church in 1636) survived destruction of the church and now stands on its own

CHURCHES

Before the Reformation the painting of churches in Scotland was usual. Afterwards it was rare, but there are two remarkable examples from the period 1630-40, one in the Skelmorlie Aisle at Largs and the other in the little church of St. Mary near Grandtully.

The Skelmorlie Aisle was built and painted for Lord Montgomery of Skelmorlie in 1636-38 and formed part of the old church of Largs until the latter was demolished in 1812. It contains an elaborate Renaissance tomb and a painted wooden vault, both without precise parallel in Scotland. The arms of Lord Montgomery, his wife and their ancestors are prominently displayed on the ceiling, together with decorative representations of Adam and Eve and Jacob and Esau, Biblical texts, the fictitious arms of the tribes of Israel, the signs of the zodiac, four paintings of the seasons and two unidentified emblematic pictures, one of which is commonly but incorrectly said to portray Lady Montgomery being kicked to death by a horse. The church at Grandtully also has a wooden vault, probably inserted when the building was repaired in 1636, and combines in somewhat similar fashion family heraldry and Biblical illustration. Both these schemes of decoration are totally different in spirit and execution from mediaeval work and neither differs significantly from secular decoration of the period.

CHURCHES: Plate 22 (*opposite*) Skelmorlie Aisle; interior. Monument to Lord Montgomery and his wife, whose coffins lie in the vault below. Plate 23 (*above*) Skelmorlie Aisle; 'Winter'. One of four scenes illustrating seasons. Plate 24 (*below*) Skelmorlie Aisle; painted timber vault which represents ribbed vault of stone, with decoration on the panels between the ribs

CHURCHES: Plate 25 St. Mary's Church, Grandtully, Perthshire. Believed to have been built before the Reformation and repaired in 1636

the Earl of Atholl and a depiction of St. Matthew

CHAPTER THREE

How the ceilings were constructed

QUEEN Mary's apartments at Holyrood have flat, timber ceilings supported by moulded ribs or coffering; ceilings of this elaborate type are also to be seen at Falkland and Kinneil but were not a feature of normal domestic architecture. The hall of a wealthy Scotsman at the beginning of the seventeenth century was still a large, moderately-lit room with paved or boarded floor, plastered walls, stone fireplace and open timber ceiling consisting of exposed joists spanning the room at intervals of about two feet and supporting both the ceiling and the walking floor of the room above. Occasionally it was spanned by no more than two or three extra-large beams, supporting smaller timbers running parallel with the side walls. The ceiling boards were tongued and grooved and nailed down onto the joists from above, but were normally not long enough to run the full length of the ceiling which had to be made up of two or three lengths mounted end to end.

The ceilings of other rooms were constructed in the same way except when allowance had to be made for the converging angle of the roof. In this case more flexible boards were used which were nailed up onto shaping pieces attached to the rafters producing a barrel vaulted or coved surface. This method was used for the great galleries at Pinkie and Earlshall.

The painters who decorated the rooms had to work on wood or plaster according to circumstances and to adjust their decoration to suit the structure of the ceiling. Flat, open-timber ceilings were divided by the joists into long

27

strips like the lights of a stained glass window; vaulted ceilings, being supported from above, could be treated as a unit, although in practice they were often marked out by the painters into smaller and more manageable areas. At Earlshall one can see the same scheme of decoration adapted to suit both the elliptical vault of the great gallery and the open-beam ceiling of the adjacent bedroom.

Most of the surviving painted ceilings are of the open-beam type partly because there were more of them originally and partly because many were retained as support for the plaster ceilings which supplanted them. Vaulted ceilings were normally destroyed, but their former existence can sometimes be deduced from the evidence of painting on the walls or from the recovery of boards re-used as lathing to support the plasterwork. Occasionally enough of such boards can be recovered to permit the reconstruction of the original painted vault, or (as at Mary Somerville's House) at least to deduce the overall pattern and subject matter of the decorative scheme.

PLATES ILLUSTRATING CHAPTER THREE

27. Holyroodhouse: coffered ceiling in Queen Mary's ante-room
28. Culross Palace: timber barrel vault. Suitable but costly way of making comfortable room beneath converging roof members
29. Kinneil House, Bo'ness, West Lothian: stone barrel vault. Plastered. Two periods of painting, one foliage, the other imitating panelling
30. Pinkie House, Loretto School, Musselburgh, Midlothian: elliptical wooden vault
31. Provost Skene's House, Aberdeen: coved ceiling. Simplest way of fitting ceiling into garret
32. Earlshall, Leuchars, Fife: elliptical vault in gallery
33. Earlshall: open timber ceiling in bedroom. Modification of decorative scheme used in gallery

shields with the arms of the queen, her husband and their families are carved as well as painted

CONSTRUCTION: Plate 28 Culross Palace: timber barrel vault. A suitable but costly way of making a comfortable room beneath converging

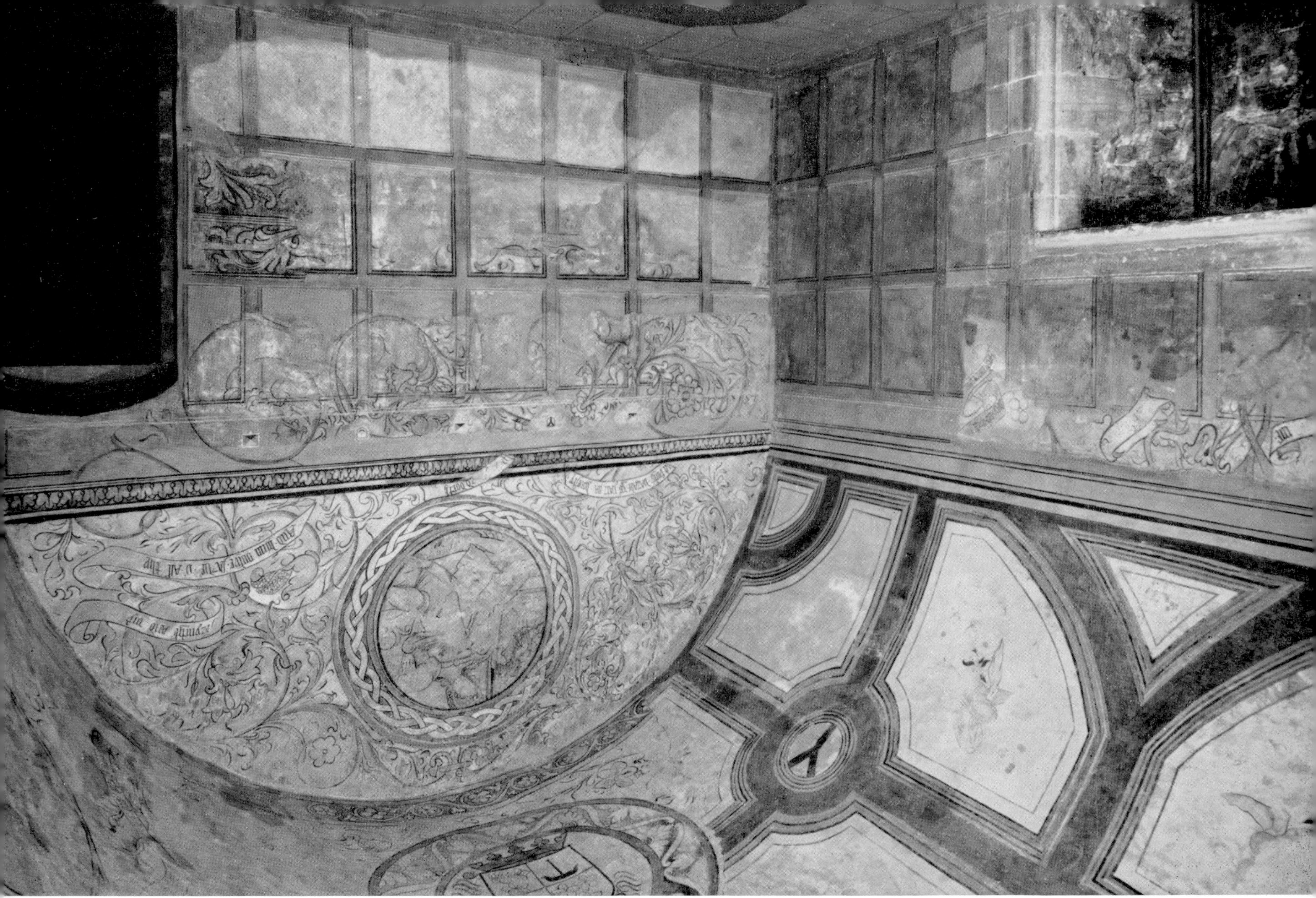

CONSTRUCTION: Plate **30** (*above*) Pinkie House, Loretto School, Musselburgh, Midlothian; elliptical wooden vault. Plate **31** (*below*) Provost Skene's House, Aberdeen; coved ceiling. The simplest way of fitting a ceiling into a garret

CONSTRUCTION: Plate 32 (*above*) Earlshall, Leuchars, Fife: elliptical vault in gallery. Plate 33 (*below*) Earlshall; open timber ceiling in bedroom. A modification of the decorative scheme used in the gallery

CHAPTER FOUR

Types of decoration

THE range of subjects used by the decorative painters was wide, but the majority can be classified under a comparatively small number of headings—floral and other patterns, classical history and mythology, grotesques, the Bible, birds and animals, emblems and heraldry. Sets of subjects such as the Seasons, the Virtues or the Senses were occasionally used and texts and proverbs, often enclosed within strap-work cartouches. Patterns, emblems and coats of arms were particularly suited to the confined spaces of the open-timber ceilings, while scenes from the Classics or the Bible were more appropriately displayed on the wider areas of walls or vaults. Simple illusionism was common—walls and partitions were 'panelled', ceilings 'coffered' and at Pinkie walls hung with 'pictures' complete with loops and nails. Vulgarity and humour are rare and there are no paintings of contemporary events. The range of beam decoration was necessarily restricted and normally confined to arabesque patterns or texts, usually enclosed in rectangles or other simple geometrical forms.

It is almost always impossible to see why people chose the decoration they did, but there are exceptions at Kirkcaldy where the beams of an old house overlooking the harbour are painted with texts referring to the sea and at Largs where the Seasons and signs of the zodiac may perhaps be regarded as appropriate to a burial aisle. Elsewhere choice was presumably governed by the taste of the patron or the ability and imagination of the painter. Whatever the motive, much of the decoration was derived from book illustrations, mostly imported from the Continent since the art of engraving was still little understood in Britain. Sometimes emblems and other devices were transferred direct from book to ceiling; more frequently they were assimilated and modified to suit the needs of the decorator. Ultimately no doubt every craftsman built up his own repertoire of decorative devices which he used according to the circumstances of the situation and which he handed down to his successors as part of his stock in trade.

PLATES ILLUSTRATING CHAPTER FOUR

34. Huntingtower: patterned ceiling
35. Northfield, Prestonpans, East Lothian: flowers and fruit
36. Northfield: ceiling survey
37. Northfield: arabesques and singing birds
38. Cullen House, Banffshire: siege of Troy
39. Crathes, Kincardineshire: Muses
40. Crathes: survey of 'Muses' ceiling
41. Prestongrange, Prestonpans, East Lothian: grotesques
42. Prestongrange: ceiling survey
43. National Museum of Antiquities, Edinburgh: Sacrifice of Isaac
44. National Museum of Antiquities: King David
45. National Museum of Antiquities: St. Luke
46. Crathes: King David
47. Mary Somerville's House: head of Christ
48. Mary Somerville's House: Agnus Dei
49. Provost Skene's House: Crucifixion
50. Kinneil: the Good Samaritan

51. Kinneil: owl
52. Lawnmarket: fox and grapes
53. Pinkie: emblem
54. Culross Palace: emblematic ceiling
55. Nunraw, East Lothian: heraldry
56. Nunraw: heraldry
57. Cullen: arms of Great Britain
58. Pinkie: painted cupola
59. Pinkie: picture of Diogenes
60. Skelmorlie Aisle: painted corbel
61. Earlshall: proverbs
62. Sailor's Walk, Kirkcaldy, Fife: Biblical texts
63. Lawnmarket: beam patterns
64. Rossend Castle, Burntisland, Fife: beam patterns
65. Rossend Castle: emblems
66. Rossend Castle: ceiling survey
67. Cologne Bible: Cain and Abel
68. John Knox House: Cain and Abel

36

side only). Décoration unique

INCHES 12   6   0   1   2   3   4   5   6   7   8   9   10 FEET

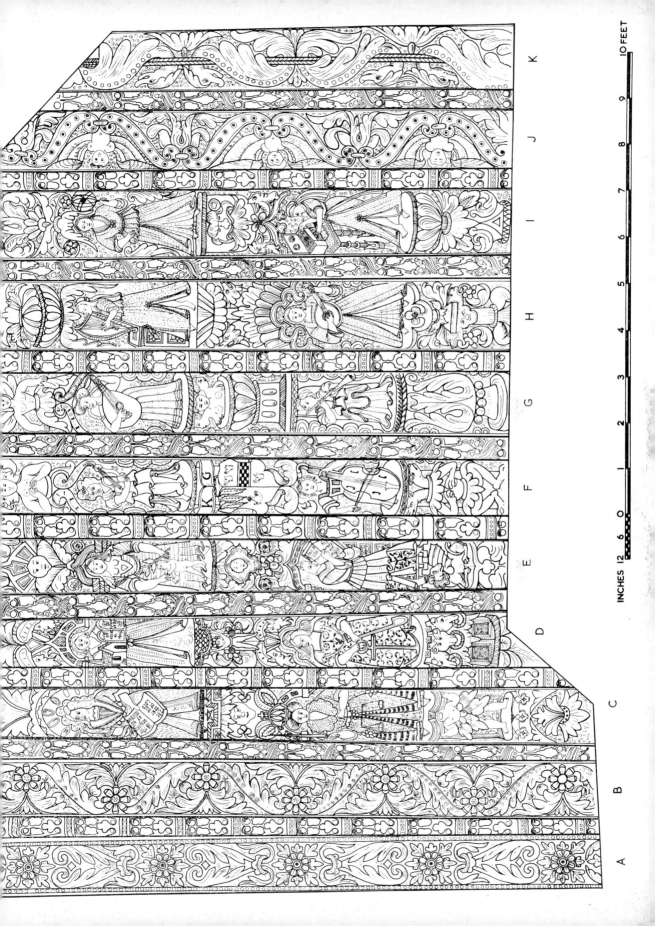

A B C D E F G H I J K

INCHES 12 6 0 1 2 3 4 5 6 7 8 9 10 FEET

Plate 42 (below) Prestongrange; ceiling survey

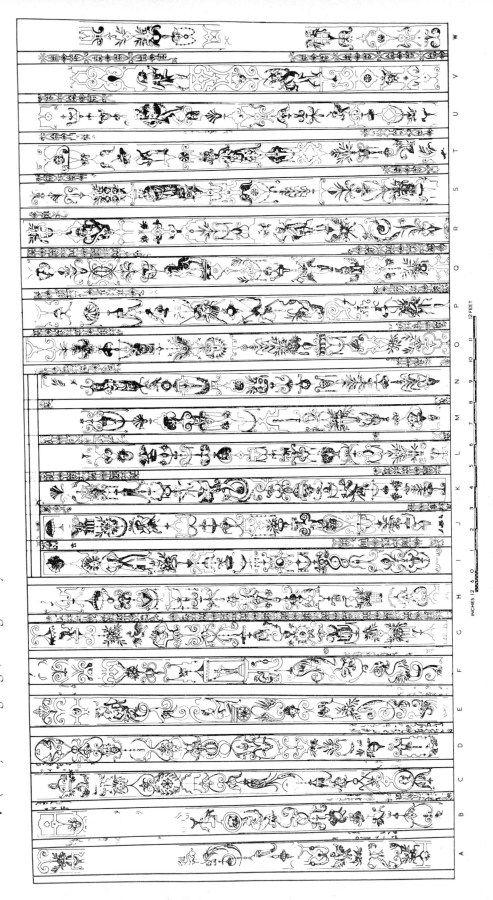

TYPES OF DECORATION: Plate **43** National Museum of Antiquities, Edinburgh; Sacrifice of Isaac. One of a series of paintings (see also Plates 44 and 45) from the Dean, an Edinburgh mansion demolished in the nineteenth century

TYPES OF DECORATION: Plate **44** National Museum of Antiquities; King David

TYPES OF DECORATION: Plate **45** National Museum of Antiquities; St. Luke

TYPES OF DECORATION: Plate **46** Crathes; King David (as one of Nine Nobles)

TYPES OF DECORATION: Plate 47 (*left*) Mary Somerville's House; head of Christ. One of a series including the Virgin Mary, Agnus Dei (see Plate 48), apostles and sibyls. Plate 48 (*above*) Mary Somerville's House; Agnus Dei (Lamb of God)

PES OF DECORATION:
posite page) Plate **50** Kinneil; the
od Samaritan. Priest and Levite pass
. One of a series illustrating the
able. Plate **51** (*above*) Kinneil; owl.
te **52** (*right*) Lawnmarket; fox and
pes

TYPES OF DECORATION: Plate 57 Cullen; arms of Great Britain. Probably an addition to the original decorative scheme

QVI SAPIT INNVMERIS MORIBVS APTVS ERIT

TYPES OF DECORATION: Plate **59** (*left*) Pinkie; picture of Diogenes. It appears to hang on the wall but in fact is painted almost horizontally on the ceiling. Plate **60** (*right*) Skelmorlie Aisle; painted corbel. The vault appears to rest on a series of corbels decorated with arms of the tribes of Israel. Plate **61** (*below*) Earlshall; proverbs

66

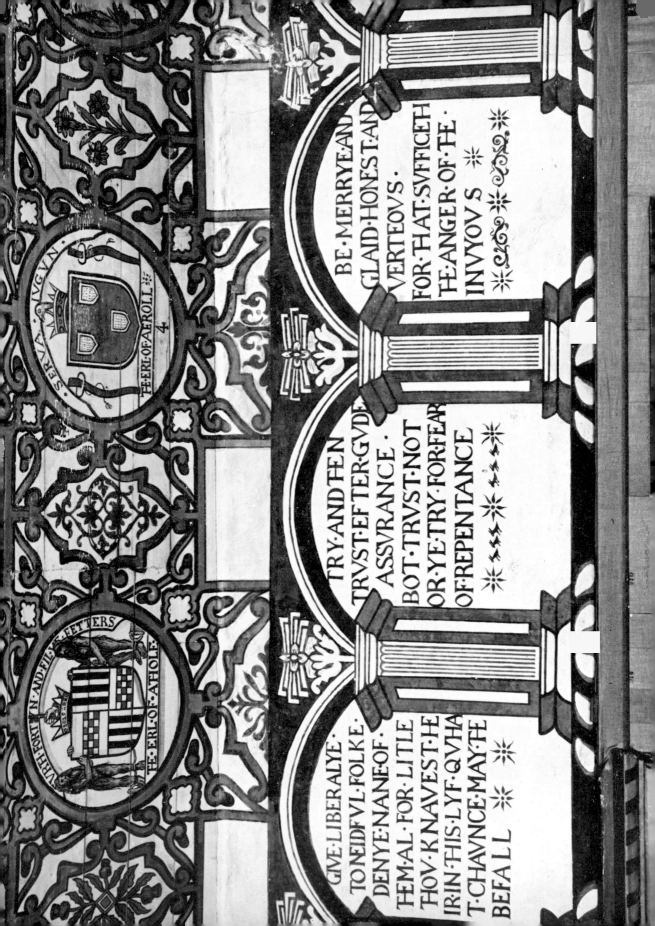

TYPES OF DECORATION. Plate 62. Sailor's Walk, Kirkcaldy, Fife. Biblical texts. 'They that go down to the sea in ships, that do business

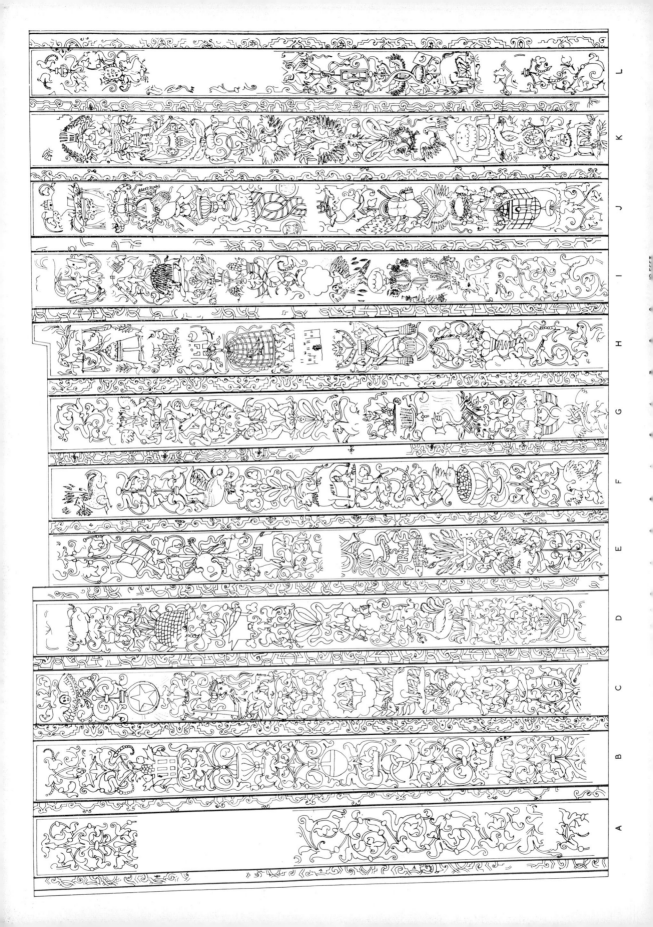

...ES OF DECORATION: Plate **66** (*opposite page*) Rossend Castle; ceiling survey. Plate **67** (*above*) Cologne Bible; ...n and Abel. One of a series of engravings produced about 1478 and frequently copied thereafter (compare Plate ... Plate **68** (*below*) John Knox House; Cain and Abel. Part of a painted ceiling, perhaps from the Dean, which ... have been inspired by the Cologne Bible. Note swans in foreground and compare Cologne Bible illustration

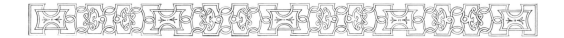

CHAPTER FIVE

Wall decoration

PAINTING on the walls was a normal part of interior decoration at the beginning of the seventeenth century, usually in association with painted ceilings. Wooden partitions in large apartments were also painted. Sometimes the painting covered the whole wall surface, but frequently it was confined to the upper part, leaving room for tapestries or hangings which excluded draughts and were both functional and decorative. Such wall decoration is often overlooked because so little survives, but traces can frequently be detected behind panelling or later plasterwork.

The most elaborate schemes of mural decoration are at Kinneil, where there is a very fine series of scenes from the Parable of the Good Samaritan. These are exceptional, appear to have been painted before 1570 and, it has been suggested, may have derived from tapestry cartoons. The adjacent vaulted chamber is also elaborately painted. Mural decoration is more commonly architectural in character, either apparently supporting the ceiling above or imitating panelling. Since the clients for whom the painting was done included the wealthy this must have been a matter of taste as well as an economy. Scenes with animals and birds were also popular, sometimes in association with Biblical texts with which they have no apparent connection.

Occasionally painted decoration preserves evidence of furnishings which formerly stood against the walls. At Culross there is structural evidence that a box bed once stood in a corner of one of the rooms in the 1611 range and this is confirmed by the fact that the decoration stops short of the area

69

which would have been concealed by the bed. The same thing can be seen in the Nine Nobles Room at Crathes and was noted at Mary Somerville's House, Burntisland, where there was evidence both of a canopied bed and of a small corner cupboard.

The Biblical and other scenes painted on the walls of houses recall the painted boards and banners which were used to decorate the streets of Edinburgh during royal processions. Thus when James VI passed through the town in 1579 'the forehouses of the streets by which the King passed were all hung with magnific tapestry, with painted histories and with the effigies of noble men and women'. Such paintings have long disappeared, but the surviving murals surely indicate what they must once have been like.

PLATES ILLUSTRATING CHAPTER FIVE

69. Gladstone's Land, Lawnmarket, Edinburgh: wall decoration

70. Kinneil: wall decoration

71. Kinneil: wall decoration

72. Traquair House, Innerleithen, Peeblesshire: wall decoration

73. Northfield: painted partition

WALL DECORATION: Plate 70 Kinneil; wall decoration. A series of Biblical scenes from the Parable Room (*below*) second period painted panelling superimposed (see Plates 29 and 105)

and bottom. The scheme originally extended right round the room. Plate 73 (above) Nolhmed, painted partition. Logs at Nolhmed and Traquair (see Plate 72 above) resemble the Scottish water hound illustrated in Conrad Gesner's *Icones Animalium* of 1560

CHAPTER SIX

When the ceilings were painted

IT is possible to say exactly when some of the ceilings were decorated because the date is painted on them; of these the earliest was at Prestongrange (1581) and the latest in the Skelmorlie Aisle at Largs (1638) with the majority of the remainder falling towards the end of the period in between. Others, as the ceiling in the royal birth chamber at Edinburgh Castle (1617), can be accurately dated from contemporary records.

In many cases it is possible to say within limits, although not precisely, when a ceiling was painted, as for example when the decoration includes the arms or monogram of the patron for whom the work was done. The decoration of the ceiling in Queen Mary's ante-chamber includes the arms of her first husband as Dauphin of France so that it must have been put up after their marriage (April 1558) and before their coronation as King and Queen of France (July 1559). At Stobhall the figure of Rex Brittanniae is a portrait of Charles I; presumably therefore the ceiling was painted between 1625 and 1648.

In every case it can be assumed that the ceiling is unlikely to be older than the building in which it is found and cannot be older than the pattern books used by the painters who painted it. The emblematic ceiling at Rossend must therefore have been painted not only after 1583 when Sir Robert Melville acquired the property, but also after 1611 when Rollenhagen first

77

published his symbolic engraving of an ostrich. It may in fact have been painted in 1616 in preparation for the visit of James VI.

Most of the remaining ceilings can be dated by comparison with one or another of the more precisely dated examples and as a result it can be said that the majority were painted between 1600 and 1650. What happened before 1600 is still obscure because although there are few known sixteenth-century examples the paintings at Kinneil show that some painted Renaissance decoration existed at least as early as 1570. Since Kinneil provides the only known example of the complete replacement of one decorative scheme by another it may be that the Kinneil paintings are earlier than those elsewhere.

Decorative painting was revived after the Civil War but on a smaller scale and in a different way. Paintings were inset into plaster ceilings or in wall panelling, particularly over the fireplaces. Sometimes the panelling itself was painted. But so far as the ceilings were concerned plaster replaced paint; thus the old decoration which had become outmoded was destroyed or concealed behind a protective layer of lath and plaster.

PLATES ILLUSTRATING CHAPTER SIX

74. Prestongrange: date on ceiling
75. Gladstone's Land: date on ceiling
76. Holyroodhouse: arms of Dauphin
77. Stobhall: Rex Brittanniae
78. Stobhall: mounted monarchs
79. Rossend Castle: part of ceiling
80. Rollenhagen's *Nucleus Emblematum Selectissimorum* 1611-13: symbol of vanity
81. Paradin's *Devises Heroiques*: symbol of Resurrection
82. Whitney's *Choice of Emblemes* 1586: symbol of ingratitude
83. Holyroodhouse: painting from Charles II's bedroom
84. Traquair House: the old library
85. Provost Skene's House: painted panelling
86. Provost Skene's House: painted panelling

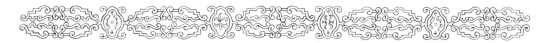

DATING: Plate 74 (*left*), Prestongrange; date on ceiling. Plate 75 (*below*) Gladstone's Land; date on ceiling

DATING: Plate 76 (above, left) Holyroodhouse; arms of the Dauphin (1558-59). Plate 77 (above, right) Stobhall; Charles I as Rex Britanniae (1625-48). Plate 78 (below) Stobhall; mounted monarchs

80

En struthium NIL PENNA juuat, quod nesciat vti :
Non PENNA EST scribas quæ facit, ipsa erit.

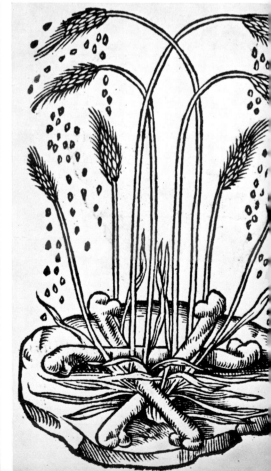

THE rauening wolfe, by kinde my mortall foe,
Yet lo, inforſde, I foſter vp her whelpe:
Who afterwarde, as it did ſtronger growe,
Thoughe as my owne, I longe the ſame did helpe:
　　Yet, coulde I not contente it with my teate,
　　But that my ſelfe, hee rent to be his meate.

No willinge minde, to pleaſe him might ſuffiſe,
No dilligence, to geue the tyraunte ſucke,
Though whelpiſhe daies, his nature did diſguiſe,
Yet time at lengthe vnto my euell lucke,
　　Bewray'de his harte, a warninge good to thoſe,
　　Whoe in theire howſe, doe foſter vp theire foes.

For, thoughe throughe neede they frendlie ſeeme a while,
Or childiſhe yeares, do cloke their cancker'd minde,
Althoughe ſome doe, releeue them in exile,
And ſpend theire goodes, in hope to alter kinde:
　　Yet all theire loue, and care to doe them good,
　　Suche will forgett, and ſeeke to ſpill theire blood.

G　　　　　GAYYH-

Nic. Reuſnerus.
*Impaſtus ſtabulis ſæuit
lupus: vbere raptos
D lamatque ſerus mi-
ſeris cum matribus
agnos.*

Claudius Minois è
Græco.
*Nutritus per me, tan-
dem fera ſamet in me.
Vertere naturam
gratia nulla poteſt.*

And. Alciat.
*Improbitas nulla flecti-
tur obſequio.*

DATING: Plate **79** (*opposite, top*) Rossend Castle; part of the ceiling. Included are initials of Sir Robert Melville and symbols from a number of identified pattern books, illustrated from the following sources: Plate **80** (*opposite, bottom left*) Rollenhagen's *Nucleus Emblematum Selectissirorum* (1611-13); symbol of vanity. The ostrich displays fine feathers, but cannot fly; Plate **81** (*opposite, bottom right*) Paradin's *Devises Heroiques;* symbol of Resurrection. The book was first published in Lyons in 1551; English edition, London 1591; Plate **82** (*above*) Whitney's *Choice of Emblemes* (1586); symbol of ingratitude. The goat suckles the wolf-cub which will eventually devour it

Plate **84** (*below*) Traquair House; the old library. Books are catalogued under the names of historians and philosophers whose portraits are painted on the cove above. Eighteenth century

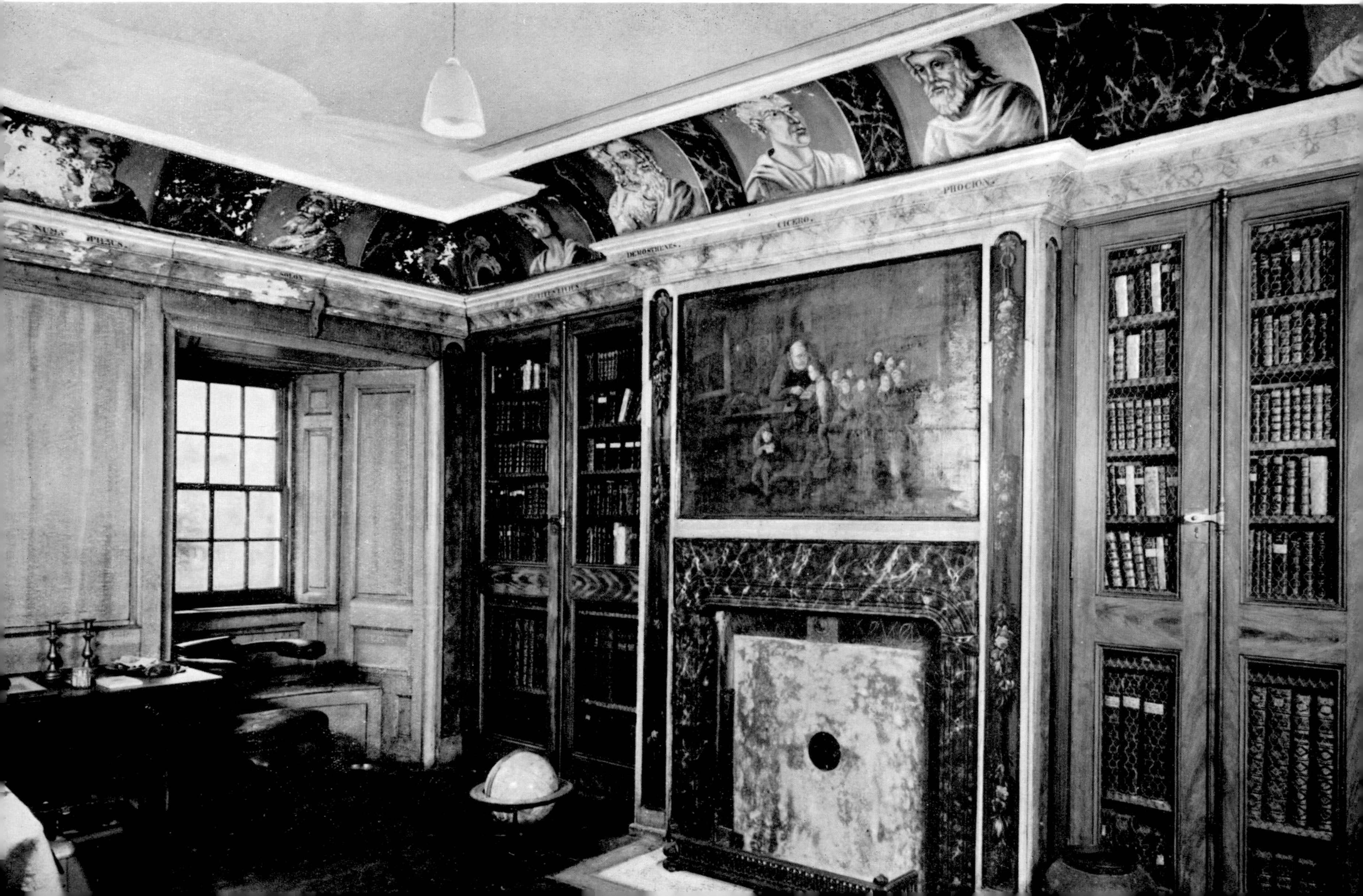

DATING: Plate **85** Provost Skene's House; painted panelling. Eighteenth century

DATING: Plate **86** Provost Skene's House; painted panelling. A detail

CHAPTER SEVEN

The painters

IT is often assumed that because painted Renaissance decoration is of foreign origin that the painters themselves were foreigners, particularly Frenchmen or Italians. This is not born out by the contemporary records which include only two outsiders, both Englishmen. Most of the work was done by local craftsmen established in Edinburgh and other towns, usually members of family firms which were handed down from father to son.

The painters of particular ceilings can occasionally be identified, notably at Largs where there is a small painted scroll in the corner of one of the paintings with the inscription 'J. Stalker fecit 1638' (J. Stalker did this in 1638). James Stalker was an apprentice in Edinburgh in 1632. A few other names have been preserved, usually in connection with payments for work done recorded in the royal or burgh accounts. John Anderson was paid £100 for painting the room in Edinburgh Castle in which the king was born and as he was summoned from Huntly to do so was presumably responsible for the emblematic paintings of which traces survive at Huntly Castle. Valentine Jenkin, one of the Englishmen, had contracts for painting at Stirling in 1628-9 so the paintings in the chapel may be attributed to him. The majority of the remaining references are to buildings or paintings which have been destroyed.

No contemporary guide to painting practice survives, but information can be obtained from the ceilings themselves. The decorators prepared their paints by mixing the pigments with glue size obtained by boiling down scraps of parchment. They then covered the ceiling with a thin coat of whiting (a mixture of chalk and size), drew out their designs on this ground with bold, black lines and finally filled in the colour. The finished painting was quite bright with a matt surface and is of a type now frequently described as tempera to distinguish it from oil painting.

Such paint is in effect a distemper and (unlike oil paint) is not waterproof. This distinction was fully understood by the decorative painters who were instructed in 1628, for example, that the 'window boards' of the king's great chamber at Stirling were to be 'layed over without with oil colour and within in temper colour'. They were also familiar with the use of red lead as a preservative for external metalwork, as at Falkland in 1629 when they were paid 'for laying over the whole iron windows with red lead and oil and for furnishing of stuff thereto'. Oil colours were used as well for heraldic painting on the outside of buildings, as also illustrated by the Stirling account of 1628 which records that the royal arms above the inner gate were to be painted 'well and sufficiently in gold and oil colours'.

PLATES ILLUSTRATING CHAPTER SEVEN

87. Skelmorlie Aisle: painting by J. Stalker

88. Chapel Royal, Stirling Castle: painting by Valentine Jenkin

89. James VI birthplace, Edinburgh Castle: painting by John Anderson

PAINTERS: Plate 88 Chapel Royal, Stirling Castle; painting by Valentine Jenkin

PAINTERS: Plate **89** Birthplace of James VI, Edinburgh Castle; painting by John Anderson

CHAPTER EIGHT

Discovery and conservation

THE existence of some painted ceilings has been known for many years but hitherto unrecorded examples continue to be discovered from time to time, sometimes as the result of an accident (as at Rossend where a stone dropped from above tore a hole in the plaster ceiling revealing painting behind) more normally through repair or demolition.

When a ceiling is first discovered and reported it is recorded. Its preservation thereafter involves conservation, for painted decoration was not intended to last for ever and both timber and paint are perishable. Sometimes very little is required, but usually timber is found to be suffering from woodworm and decay, while pigments have been reduced to little more than a powder.

The problems of conservation are well illustrated at Culross and Kinneil. At Culross boards found stacked in piles and out of context were cleaned of whitewash, disinfected in a gas chamber, made good and re-assembled in their original positions on the evidence of the post holes cut in the floor. At Kinneil, where the paintings were revealed by demolition, the timber ceiling was retrieved from the breaker's yard and two complete rooms rehabilitated, in one case in such a way as to illustrate two different schemes of decoration.

Conservation raises technical problems. Since nearly every ceiling in Scotland has received treatment at some time or other allowance must be made for this as well as for the effects of age. The paintings were originally much brighter and gayer than they are today. In spite of this they preserve enough of their original colouring and spirit to illustrate the technical and artistic merit of the original design.

PLATES ILLUSTRATING CHAPTER SIX

90. Rossend Castle: discovery of ceiling

91. Rossend Castle: discovery of ceiling

92. Rossend Castle: the ceiling exposed

93. Mary Somerville's House: discovery of ceiling

94. Mary Somerville's House: lathing exposed

95. Lawnmarket: discovery of ceiling

96. Lawnmarket: ceiling exposed

97. Culross Palace: boards in gas chamber

98. Culross Palace: whitewash partly removed

99. Culross Palace: room without painted boards

100. Culross Palace: framing for painted partition

101. Culross Palace: reconstruction complete

102. Kinneil: north wing at time of discovery

103. Kinneil: Arbour Room at time of discovery

104. Kinneil: Parable Room at time of discovery

105. Kinneil: plasterwork at time of discovery

OVERY AND CONSERVATION: Plate 90 (*above*) Rossend Castle; discovery of ceiling (1957). The first floor hall
he of discovery. Plate 91 (*below*) Rossend Castle; discovery of ceiling. The painting is revealed behind plaster

DISCOVERY AND CONSERVATION: Plate 93 (*above*) Mary Somerville's House; discovery of ceiling. Strips of painted lathing are exposed by removal of partitions. Plate 94 (*below*) Mary Somerville's House; lathing exposed. Ancient painted lathing was recovered to permit reconstruction of the ceiling

DISCOVERY AND CONSERVATION: Plate 97 (*above, left*) Culross Palace; boards in gas chamber. Plate 98 (*above, right*) Culross Palace; whitewash partly removed. Plate 99 (*below*) Culross Palace; room without painted bo.

RECOVERY AND CONSERVATION: Plate 100 (*above*) Culross Palace; framing for painted partition. Plate 101 (*below*) Culross Palace; reconstruction complete

DISCOVERY AND CONSERVATION: Plate **102** (*above*) Kinneil; north wing at time of discovery (1936). Plate **103** (*below*) Kinneil; Arbour Room at time of discovery. Note grooves cut to support later panelling (See Plates 29 and 71)

DISCOVERY AND CONSERVATION: Plate 104 (*above*) Kinneil; Parable Room at time of discovery (see Plate 70). Plate 105 (*below*) Kinneil; plasterwork at time of discovery. The painted plaster surface is prepared to support secondary plasterwork which concealed it

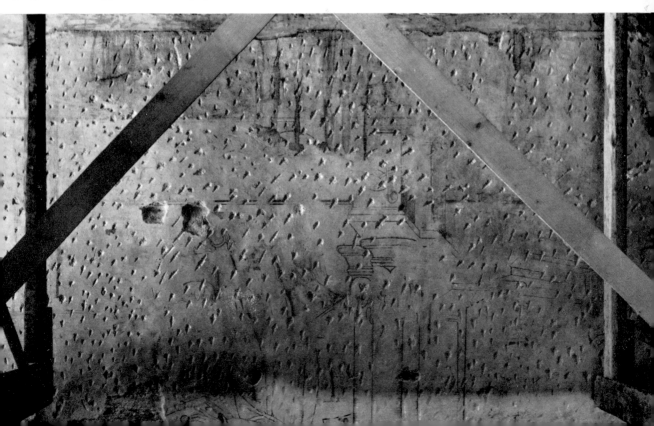

Come unto mee, all yee that are weary and laden, and I will ease you. Matth. 11. 28

Take heed to thy foot when thou entrest into the house of God, & be more neere to heare then to give the sacrifice of fooles. Eccle. 5.1

Precious in the sight of the Lord is the death of his saints. Psal. 116. 15

Index

Printed in Scotland for Her Majesty's Stationery Office by George Outram & Co. Ltd., Perth

Wt. 72100 K24

S.O. Code No. 67-240*

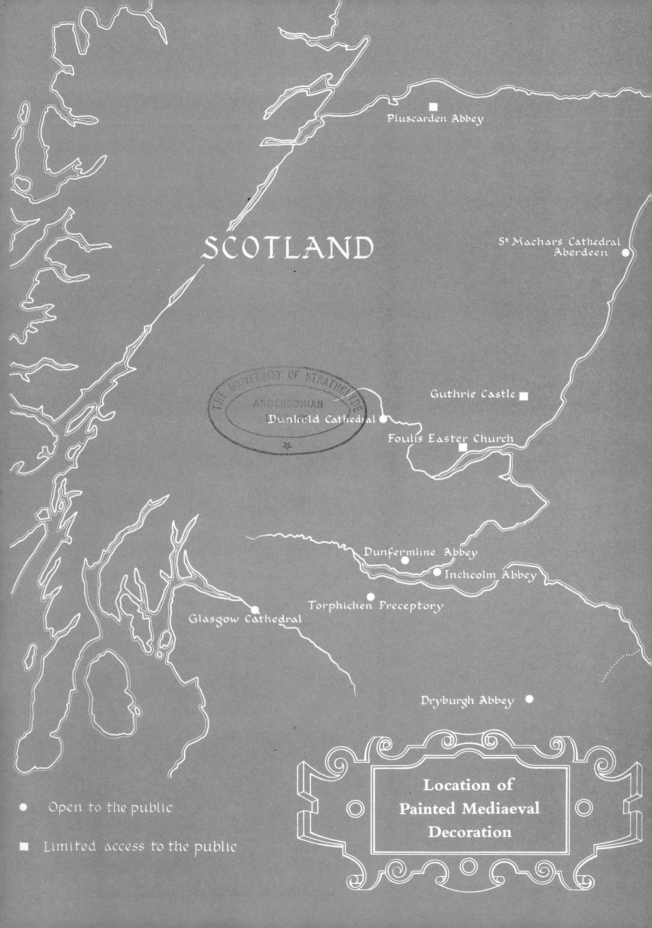

SCOTLAND

Pluscarden Abbey

St Machars Cathedral
Aberdeen

Guthrie Castle

Dunkeld Cathedral

Foulis Easter Church

Dunfermline Abbey

Inchcolm Abbey

Torphichen Preceptory

Glasgow Cathedral

Dryburgh Abbey

● Open to the public

■ Limited access to the public

Location of
Painted Mediaeval
Decoration